ASPHALT

ASPHALT

Rebekah Remington

Winner of the Harriss Poetry Prize
Michael Salcman, Prize Series Editor
Marie Howe, 2013 Contest Judge

CITYLIT
PRESS

Baltimore, Maryland

Library of Congress Control Number: 2013949123
ISBN 978-1-936328-15-4
CityLit Project is a 501(c)(3) Nonprofit Organization
Federal Tax ID Number: 20-0639118
Printed in the United States of America
First Edition

Book Design: Nathan Rosen
and Gregg Wilhelm
Cover Art: Carolyn Case
Blue vs. Blue, 2011
Oil on panel
12x12 inches
© Carolyn Case

CITYLIT
PRESS

c/o CityLit Project
120 S. Curley Street
Baltimore, MD 21224
410.274.5691
www.CityLitProject.org
info@citylitproject.org

For Stephen

Contents

Introduction

I was very moved by many of the manuscripts I read, but I could not stop thinking of Rebekah Remington's collection, *Asphalt*.

The voice in these poems is so true to an actual living voice: a woman thinking aloud in the way of women. The metaphysical gets mixed up with the toys still strewn on the floor and the inner voices threaten to drown out the day. This gorgeous persistence, this exultant surrender, and all of it happening in the mess of what we call the "everyday." It is spoken in a voice so witty, charming, self-infuriated, and fierce ("Remind yourself you've never been pretty/ could never hear iambs, how as a child you watched/ hours of the stupid genie on TV and the fruition/ of wishes inevitably led to a night in the slammer"). I come back to this voice as to a friend whose company feels essential.

Perhaps the most moving theological/political/exploratory poetry is indeed being written in the car on the way to the liquor store, or standing in the living room "In praise of the last hour of the afternoon." There's a charity in the gaze of these poems and a language rich with the felt life of every living thing.

> *In September my son writes an essay called "Brave Boy"*
> *and the teacher calls his handwriting sloppy.*
> *The vagabond stands on the green island*
> *and the light changes.*

I love how Remington's mind moves from this to that to this in some utterly lived syllogism ("What looks like failure is something else"). I love how the poet—desperate as the rest of us (Shock Top, Raging Bitch, Blue Motion/ Something for the afternoon, when the children/ mine for virtual diamonds/ How do I get a pickaxe?/ Press B)—loves the world: "The bees come. The apples."

Marie Howe
New York State Poet Laureate
New York, NY

Little Invocation

Don't open the blinds; give me fifteen minutes.

This morning my mind like a century
which sees the rise and fall of 22 emperors
and all I've done is empty the dishwasher.

Grant me a sweet cup of forgetfulness, God.

Let's blot out the never-made call to the lonely friend.
The baby sunflower, gift from my son, I didn't water
four days in a row.

Once I wrote a twenty-page paper delineating
all the muscles bones tracts synapses involved in speaking
the word *spring*.

Envision a wild system of estuaries, derivations,
deer skeleton, river thaw,
the road to the contagious hospital.

Now say it aloud.

61 Keys

A keyboard, like the one we owned,
is no piano. It had a trumpet mode,
a harp mode, a mode that sounded like a coughing dog.
Often, out of boredom or helplessness, I don't know which,
my son would switch timbres mid-song.
It had a mode like bicycle wheels after rain.

The overpass construction went on and on,
ripping out wildflowers planted on the exit ramp,
turning the air bright with dust.
Once where the flowers had been
we watched a spot-a-pot installation.
A few days later a black crane rose like a Brancusi bird
I'd seen in *Janson's History of Art*.

No roads closed, traffic too vital to stop.
Each Friday afternoon we would cross
the bridge on foot, my son and I, for his piano lesson.
In winter we were hard to see.
As far as I know, no one ever jumped from the bridge.
Such a death could easily involve a stranger.

Should I say that was the year I stopped bleeding
or the year I heard a cloud around which the air
formed itself into cicada, C scales, and jackhammer crescendo—
oh loveliness of hands, of experience,
oh pearl-like loveliness of a single hour—
the year of the bridge renovation,
the year of *Mozart Made Easy for Piano?*

In Praise of the Last Hour of the Afternoon

The afternoon's yours: silence, rain, milk left out
    in a glass, and the unswept tile,
        and derailed toy trains.

The afternoon's an island, miles of theoretical coastline, a long walk
    in the mind, soldier apparitions pocketing limestone,
        part fish, part dream shard, spine bone

to finger and translate in the dissolving day. If the catalpa moves in the wind
    is that enough? If one walks the perimeter once more?
        In the material world muffled cues are everywhere:

the unplayed Ode to Joy open on the music stand,
    remotes and geodes on the coffee table,
        the breeze on the glass erotic almost.

Your mother's life a hairsbreadth different from your own.
    The little plastic throwaways from China, for instance.
        She never had this problem.

You think sun blooms on the Yellow River Basin.
    You think but don't know.
        You're in another country.

You're like any mother. You'd trade pearls for quiet
    before the children rush in with their end-of-the-day edginess
        their hunger their reports of small injustices.

You go for a bottle of Red Truck, pellucid and plum-colored.
    Make note to note your beloved's eyes:
        graphite flecked with onyx and snapdragon,

the underside of a waterfall. You live in a time of war.
    The President has kept the coffins hidden.
        In the corner of your vision a city burns.

And the little birds eat seed cake and are next to nothing.
And the shadows have their say.
And the oval track in your living room remains.

Goat

The weather was saying come out and so they did,
the man, the woman, the boy, adjusting to the waning heat
after so much midday sun, after the inertia of indoors,
the blare of screens, the sticky floor, the fragile
arrangement of trains.
       The boy kept falling off his bicycle,
getting back on, pedaling the short length of the field.
It was a return to kindness, despite the gnats everywhere
like colliding names coming out of the future.
It was a reprieve after so much flickering noise.
Beyond the baseball diamond, at the far edge of the complex,
a goat walked to a fence, waiting to be fed
milk thistle or burdock or a graham cracker
from the hands of the child, who imagined he alone
had been born for this moment, that without him
the goat might die of hunger or loneliness.
The sky had taken on a shapeliness like a flood plain
in an aftermath, an eerie pinkish erasure.

Happiness Severity Index

Though in the lower standard deviation, I fall, the statistician says,
within the normal range of happiness. Therefore, no drugs today.

What about tomorrow? What if doodling stars isn't enough?
Will I be asked to color the rainbow one more time?

Name three wishes that might come true?
List everything I've been given within a minute?

Though within the normal range of happiness, I score poor
on bird appreciation, poor on oboe joy. My responses, in fact,

seem to indicate an overall confusion concerning joy itself.
What did I mean that during parties I choose the sofa

like a sick cat? That when tattoos are dispensed I'm first
in line? That books full of other people's misery

make the beach infinitely more pleasant? Stargazing is another weakness.
Too much I examine the patch of dirt where nothing grows

where buried curiosa aren't deep enough, though in Short Answer
I'm all for dancing alone in a silken robe. Friends call.

Mostly the machine answers. Mozart makes me cry.
I kill spiders without guilt. To make up for this

I take the kids to the golden arches play area.
A positive indicator. Also, interest in the existential

is minimal. I approve of make-up and ice cream.
When I wake early, I get out of bed. When I wallow

in planetary counterpoint, it never lasts. And here's what
really saves me: if I were a ghost I'd be Casper. If I were a tradition

I'd be a dreidel. I like the rain. When the boat drifts off
I wave. When the dog runs off I follow.

I Call Her Inez

The speaker in the video, in black, said picture an attendant spirit
when you draw or write. That way it's not all on you.
You feel enough failure as it is

by your streaky window that should house a houseplant,
but doesn't. Get a pencil. Glass of chardonnay.

I see her now, fifteen minutes after the hour.
She carries a mason jar full of shadows,

shakes them out across the floor.
They blow into corners like Thing 1 and Thing 2.

It's true I love shadows, she knows this.
One has ghost-blue eyes like my mother's mother.

One smells like formaldehyde.
Shadow fingers pull a shadow IV.

My attendant has slept alone in a tent just below the timber line
but cannot name one mountain flower.

She won't talk about the summit, what the clouds said,
but tells how a man stumbled on his way down

muttering how his son disappeared into radioactive
sky, the discolored photo on the post office wall.

She knows how to spell *grotesque* and *grandiose* but not *grateful.*
She has never been to Reykjavik, but brings
twice-baked potatoes from south Baltimore,

a remedy parcel from a strip-mall drugstore. Take. Eat.
The hereafter's quiet as an empty auditorium.

The sun drove her to delirium once in a fishing boat.
It was like being inside a man.

History of in-house detention. History of truancy.
Cheater at Scrabble, muse of half-lies.

No body, no heavy periods.
Once she convinced eleven others to put a man in jail.

He calls me sometimes, after she's gone. Describes a Texan sunset
through wire, the recantation of seven witnesses, a drunken defender.

Adulterations of the Inner Ear

A noise like crying, a woman
in the after-midnight night,
perhaps from the house of foreigners
perhaps stumbling southward from the 7-11
after having been shoved from a rusty Malibu
then invited back in, but it's summer, not too hot,
so she walks, wanders, city-ward
toward screeching, wine, tangles of sleeping children.
If I had to guess I'd say she loves bangles
has had wire under her breasts for a very long time.
She knows isolated passages from Isaiah
and complicated recipes from the Himalayas.
Yes, she has given birth, but that was years ago.
The cries come from the direction of the rhododendron
where once a robin built a sturdy nest
then abandoned it after a week.
I took the desertion personally
like the dying of neighbor's betta
left in my care during the holiday.
How sickly still the fish in ornamental lights
until I banged the glass and he yielded
with a paltry quiver.
It would not be hard to find her, the woman.
It is a small yard with hedges in the back.
It would not be hard to find her now
that the Paradise Tavern has closed.
She is crouched like a large stone.
She has wandered east, I think,
from the state hospital when the guard
turned his eyes to dial a girl,
wandered east with purposelessness

or the purpose of a dragonfly.
Her mind is a meadow. She wants to alight.
She is any intricacy—of mystery, of hunger.
I tire of her difficulties. The night is any night,
full of vexation, rat-like shadows, elsewhere
rhapsodies. The odor of hydrangea
fills the world. A melange of throat noise
rises, indistinguishable as colors in the dark,
drifts, taken back into something resembling pure sound,
traffic whir and a thousand bird songs.

Halo Dialogues Ending in Funambulism

Transfiguration is too much for people like us,
*   we could never make sense of such things*

       she said as we passed Bertamini's salon.
Through the tattooed glass

    we could see Iris twirl her curling brush
       through beetle-brown strands.

In the back a row of widows browsed the glossies.
    In the end nothing is ever fine enough

       without some kind of supernatural noonday finish.
In those days my friend and I had many such conversations,

    quasi-religious, not without faith exactly,
       but with no pretense of authority

or care to convince, a queer kind of meandering
    between diapers and feedings about the good,

       the difficult, or the woman's body as a thing apart.
Where we walked a canopy of black walnut

    made swathes of light on the road that
       wound past the old rich houses,

front yards of brambles and stylized dandelions.
    The roll of stroller wheels lulled the babies.

She said, *I saw this woman in a candy shop.*
 I could not stop staring. Have you never felt mythically beautiful?

I remembered before thirteen, no, ten,
 perhaps then, perhaps never

perhaps when I thought of nothing
 but fields and horses I would never own.

 Yet the cries of the babies contained, I thought,
all the beauty in the world, though they too,

 would learn ungainliness. *What is certain,* she said,
 is soup kitchen work. We went on

to argue the worthiness of tightrope walking.
 Height and peril is everything,

   spurning the law, creating a murmur
below the cypress. I don't care how many spires you bridge.

 The crowd can't stop looking up,
  those who want it to happen, those who don't.

Little Seismic

I was there.
The fan trembled.
The plant trembled.
The rented room became one faint undulation.

Great Aunt Mary said, "I think we should go."

Outside, the sun reigned.
The sand was as usual. Bright umbrellas.
Women in tankinis, their happy and unhappy bodies,
walking along, and the ocean liners far off, unshaken.

Later we bought a six pack and a bag of groceries.
"Did you feel it?" a stranger in line asked.

The National Cathedral, a place I have visited only twice,
lost three pinnacles off its central tower.

What else? Nothing else, or this:
the bees come, the apples.

In September my son writes an essay called "Brave Boy,"
and the teacher calls his handwriting sloppy.

The vagabond stands on the green island,
and the light changes.

Why do the bees sound so happy this year?
Why are the houses all awake,
shining lights even in daylight?

The anti-confessional prodigal daughter
goes about her business, filing papers, buying groceries.

When I stand in the white glow of the refrigeration zone
in Paradise Liquors it's the names I love:

Flying Dog, Resurrection, Woody Creek.

It's not all about high alcohol content.

Shock Top, Raging Bitch, Blue Motion.

Something for the afternoon, when the children
mine for virtual diamonds.
How do I get a pickaxe?
Press B.

The bees come. The apples.

Snow and Din

Another night of the beautiful investigators
questioning me, writing it down.
The absence of a body means nothing.
Snow covers so much.
While the man sweet talks, the woman produces
a photograph, wound the size of a damson.
Her compassion for wronged animals
should be a comfort, but isn't.
Hadn't I seen anything in the halogen light?
Hadn't I heard the scratching in the cellar?
I am acting the part of an amateur,
gray roots beginning to show
like the woman who works the graveyard shift
at the supermarket,
who has mastered exhaustion
though not dissembling.
What's the difference between flaw
and sin? Drinking light beer in a boat, for instance,
three children, two life jackets,
the heat like a laundromat in August.
Indifference is a sin. Reading can be
if someone's feverish and needs a drink of water.
I swear the hours were all about cryptograms.
I saw no one. No one saw me.
The old man who bought the elixir
was someone in a dream.
The male investigator says something in French,
something about spring,
purple blossoms diseasing the cracks.
After their exit, it's like the rest of
any night, sleeping pills,
loose dogs barking at the town's edge.

Wanting

When the woman took her to the Payless
to find the sparkling crimson slippers, advertised in a paper
among flip-flops, rhinestone boots, and mary janes, the girl
fell in love with a pair of black flats she swore fit
though they didn't and were out of price range;
they resembled the ones the young Chinese servant wore,
the one who had endured many unjust whippings
in an American film the girl had seen four times,
enough to fancy a life under feudal strictures,
where each afternoon she must bring tea to the mistress
thick with opium on an opium-induced shore.

On Hunger

Because you need to eat you see the tabloids.
Because you need milk and oranges in cans, light syrup.
This night all the stories about the body about fatigue.
All the stories about fatigue about the body.
Because your children need to eat.
Because he says you're beautiful and you can't believe him.
Because the tabloids love mockery more than execution.
And maybe, too, because, everything can be found
aisle after aisle, you fall in—
cornflakes, apple, little bottle of Aubade for the nails.
Your walk under fluorescence a sleep walk

but containing also,
as in most sleep, a remembering:
water breaking on your thighs, then quickening cold,
sun spangle, the other swimmers, the distance
the light traveled to reach you.
Do you forget the hour spent in spindrift?
Was that indifference?

Air

Days when I think I have come as far
as the tomatoes in the Shop & Save,
pithy, tasteless, forever unripe,
hauled across a thousand miles of desert

I am still grateful for the air.

It offers no moral but let's me sit and drink my coffee.

Question: would a plastic bag work
or do you you need pills too?

Is the air too seductive for a would-be suicide?

Barely enough for the asthmatic

to a child it's the only thing that can't be seen.
Even God is more visible, even a moon flower.

I have seen it invent love in smoky juke joints.

Filled with the scent of carrion,
filled with the scent of huckleberry

it draws bears and wolves into the clearing.

In an empty recital hall it feels somehow altered,
heavy-light, streaming, expectant,
as if even grief might not be what it seems,

a heroine under brown pond water,
an unmoving surface,

a vanishing into—

Asphalt

Another crash on the onramp set me to thinking about lying to children
or not lying about the Buddha.
Saying, that girl died because she didn't wear a seatbelt.
She's in heaven now, I think.
How do you know if you lie?
Dean once said, "I'll believe anything if you sing it."
Beauty is truth and truth beauty wobbling in the anti-gravity chamber.
At seventeen, severe acne. The doctor's word: Severe.
At forty, at the ultrasound: There's no heartbeat. There's just you.
What if I can't sing?
Elephants don't fly. My grammar twists. A boy calls me ugly.
Another crash on the onramp set me to thinking about a movie
full of crashes, a man and a woman stumbling along the highway
in the night
passing mangled vehicle after mangled vehicle.
A man and a woman unable to speak. Not speaking.
Another crash on the onramp
reminded me of the Lutheran neighbor who said the National Cemetery
is a good place to walk,
then the next day, No, probably not for a woman alone with a baby.
Another crash reminded me of an edgy poem with an edge of light
(someone walking away this time, trembling but unscathed).
Not moonlight, not the tortured light of a man drinking whiskey alone
but dawn-gray light, light that seeps under the door at 6 am,
kids clashing in the corridor,
and a newspaper, something to stop the nightly ruminations,
news not too bad.
What's the truth anyway? I'm not one to get too semantic.
I prefer a window view, sitting cross-legged with a cup of tea.
See that lot with the crumbling asphalt?
I like that.

School Morning

Daily rehearsal for good-bye, I think,
because I am a pessimist by nature.

I think salmon going upstream,
I think the elusive city, long-distance static interference,
time zone difference.

I think rough-boy surreptitious blow. Bully.

Because I'm an average or maybe below-average mother
I think thank you jesus.

Because I want to make a poem which contains the Badlands.

Because I want to raise a respectable citizen:
No, I won't carry your bag.

The bus arrives like a black-eyed susan in the fog.
It is a yellow cell of pathos and transport
to quadratic equations, legible alphabets, arms waving pick me.

Dodgeball, thumbtacks, monotony.
Recruiters.
Someone vomiting in the library.
Free trombone lessons and a band to boot.

My older son waves from a long row of windows.
My younger flaps down the moving aisle,
no longer sees me.

Then I am alone in the weed-choked house.
The rain is about to come and there are dishes to unload.
Hello, notebook and pencil. Empty pastures
of sky. Something stirring
in the rocks that won't be seen.

Because the closest I came to divine rubble was holding a baby.

Later, I will kneel and pick up small things,
merge the LEGOs, recycle origami swans.
Later, I will hack the wild vines.
In some stories the bus is a chariot pulled by six black horses.
Good-bye to the girl in the copacetic meadow.

In some stories, the yellow bus has wings.
Cacophony shooting through the cosmos.
No one strapped in.
Some small cruelty taking place near the back.

Fully Half Full

This isn't the loveliest I've ever been.
I grow brutish about the clutter.
Still the liquid in the glass grows visible,
fizzy, reminiscent of a not-so-weary river.
I've yet to see a sacred goat but even that seems possible.
8.3% ale helps. So too poetry.
In poetry sadness sells
not unlike explosions on the screen
not unlike tricks on ice.
The girl dressed like a bluebird.
Once I met a guy who swore he'd never been sad.
Not really. Photos of the first monkeys
in space filled him with hope. All the Alberts
dead before impact and still the moon in his ken.
That said, let's go watch the acting students walk the plank.
Our sons won't love a pirate ship forever.
Let's pick up a cake in the shape of a steam engine,
puffs of gray sugar exhaled in the upper left.

October Divide

Joe-Pye-weed pushing
through during the reign
of the scarecrow.

Cedarwood, Elm, Prospect.
I pass a litter of toddler cars, bright and deserted,
a tulle ghost hanging from a rafter.

I pass a retirement chair outside a retirement garden.
60% chance of sun
and no sun. A gnarled man looks up.

The sky is all steeples and billboards.
This one for the Human Systems exhibit,
authentic dead hearts moving city to city.

This one for the fuel fund.
I'm going for espresso
in a heated car, part of me

in love with red and gold
descending. The other part
has turned in the theology books,

turned off the war news,
in league with every jack-o'-lantern
squirrel-gnawed and blue-black.

Forty

Remind yourself you've never been pretty,
could never hear iambs, how as a child you watched

hours of the stupid genie on tv and the fruition
of wishes inevitably led to an night in the slammer,

IRS at the door, woman sleeping in a bottle.
Switch channels: detergent, white noise, car off a cliff.

Remind yourself your children are lovely.
You can still get tickets for the open-air bus,

the hop-on, hop-off pigeon-sighting circuit
that operates in winter and cyclonic winds.

You'll wear a rain poncho like all the others.
You'll notice the man shivering in the doorway,

the faux mask vendor, odor of garlic and exhaust
rising. You'll notice as well the midtown

giantess in whom no one believes, her flat
shiny belly selling younger and richer

and red rivulet hair. She's as poignant as
barbed wire, so you want her there the way

you want a coelacanth in your next poem
or the one after that, something trying to swim

out of depths but it can't or won't.
It becomes a lyric, or the name, at least,

for an amateur band, lead guitarist's face
gashed with accentual scars.

Remind yourself you're four hours from New York.
You've seen the pink shit sculptures.

You still wonder what the soul is.

Fish Hunting

Listen to the rain outside the House of Tropicals.
We came to build a landscape, so many ruins to choose from,

so many castles. The three of us walked aisles of tanks,
dollar danios straight from heaven.

The child asked if the highwayman would appear in the nights.
He was, I think, speaking of pain.

There was enough painted gravel to make a coastline,
stones that shone like sun-lost swimmers.

The clerk swore she loved every fish
though only some were emissaries.

First Week at P.S. 33

We read the cumulatives, turned the desks. A voice on the loudspeaker
said report to the cafeteria to pick up your kit.
How pairs of dragonflies made an operatic difference
imperative to survival was the first lesson. An assistant
said here's another transfer from 48. A boy. A voice

said report to the cafeteria to pick up your kit.
Inside: a bottle of Purell and list of emergency numbers
imperative to survival. Was the first lesson an assistant
in black overalls, speaking a dialect, playing the bells?
Or did it involve no shows, throwing water near the water cooler?

Inside: a bottle of Purell and list of emergency numbers
we might find necessary should a child elope.
In black overalls, speaking a dialect, playing the bells,
the teacher led the children to believe Thursday would be different.
It was boiling in there but there was nowhere else.

January Morning

Inevitable the denuded conifer blowing across the road.
Inevitable, water into stone— yet

when I say winter, picture solstice, wine, the return
of sun to the subzero outskirts.

Picture an ice pick tossed aside.
A bowl of Moroccan clementines.

Here: radiator, flannel, our bodies lit,
fingers tracing wristlet vines.

You've missed the commuter train.
Let's linger, let brilliance rush the gap of bedroom

door latched with hook and eye.
Hear the children leap mattress to mattress.

They refuse to change from superhero jammies
and gather their school things.

When I say cold I mean outside.
Here: scent like a pine forest,

shepherds bewildered as ever,
knee-high in brittle greenery and tinsel strands.

Break into my spent marrow.

Sunday Return

The sun was out and the moon was out.
The boys were a thousand miles off.
I purchased rubber band flying machines.
I liked my body when I was with alone and
I liked my body when I thought of them.
My difficult body.

In the photo they sent I could see the mess
in the living room, the one that I would enter
the way I might enter a messy myth,
the children butterflying in the municipal pool,
the man reciting mandolin Spanish.
In my marrow what had opened was hailstorm,
a flying branch, crushed honeysuckle.

The way home was five mountain ranges,
eleven states, three time zones.
The way home was a milky way of blackbirds.
The way home was strung out flares, unshoeing,
the lonely slots of Reno.
In earlier times many died crossing that distance.

Ghost Birds and Horizontal Plummet

Baling wire, yellow feather, hunk of wood:
    glued and soldered
    fraught form
        in motion and not in motion
    first seen in a studio
hanging glad-hearted, yellow of the sun-
                    flower feather
is the poem I wanted to write.

Emerging from the grime
    to the street buskers to the galleries
        became an absolute good
    even in a rain storm
    even after a break up.
The coke addict who taught me chess
    could not teach me to fly.
        Falling became an existence, and yet
the hellbent holy spirit spinning feather spun.

The poem called "Failure" is a dog without a sense of smell
running through a cornfield.

In Iowa I lost a baby
    (before that babies came easy, without charts).
    What I remember about Iowa:
        the bird center with the broken birds,
        words etched in the sidewalk.
    I lost a baby there and wrote about it.
    Nobody had a clue.
    It was a bad post-modern miscarriage poem,
        lots of blood and no back story. No front story either.

The poem called "Beginnings" opens with a child in a cemetery.

Most I've my life I've lived in small towns.
The yellow feather and the hunk of wood in the third bedroom.
There's a lot of chess and yelling in the streets.
There's a lot of making up.
All through the house the pencils are breaking.
Lots of groceries, lots of wine, lots of toy guns.
I met my best friend in a small town.
She paints weavings with sudden brown splotches
when she's not mothering or discussing her mother.
She took me on a bus once to see Marina Abramovic.
What looks like failure
is something else I meant to tell you:
the naked body hurling itself repetitively into a wall.

Acknowledgments

Grateful acknowledgement is made to the editors of the following journals, in which these poems appeared:

Bellingham Review Online:
"In Praise of the Last Hour of the Afternoon"
"I Call Her Inez"

Blackbird:
"Little Invocation"

Gargoyle:
"Forty"

Hayden's Ferry Review:
"Halo Dialogues Ending in Funambulism"

Interrupture:
"Adulterations of the Inner Ear"
"Sunday Return"

Linebreak:
"Little Seismic"

The Missouri Review:
"Goat"

Ninth Letter:
"First Week at P.S. 33"

Rattle:
"The Happiness Severity Index"

Smartish Pace:
"October Divide"

I am grateful to the Maryland State Arts Council, the Rona Jaffe
Foundation, the Bread Loaf Writers' Conference, the Squaw Valley
Community of Writers, and the Gettysburg Review Writers' Conference
for scholarships and awards that supported the writing of these poems.

I'm also indebted to the members of Frank Bidart's workshop at the
New York State Summer Writers Institute for their friendship, attentive
readings, and encouragement. Thanks to my teachers and mentors.
Many family members and friends provided emotional support,
especially Bernadine Remington, Elizabeth Remington, Andrew
Remington, Laura Golberg, and Marianne O'Leary. Thanks to Carolyn
Case without whose friendship and constant encouragement this book
would not exist.

Love to Stephen, Max, and Emmett. Thanks for your boundless
patience.

Finally, my deep gratitude to Marie Howe for selecting my
manuscript, and to Gregg Wilhelm and everyone at CityLit Project who
made this book possible.

About the Poet

Rebekah Remington holds a BA from The Johns Hopkins University and an MFA from the University of Michigan. Her poetry has appeared in *Linebreak*, *The Missouri Review*, *Ninth Letter*, *Bellingham Review Online*, *Hayden Ferry's Review*, *Smartish Pace*, and elsewhere. She is the recipient of two Maryland State Arts Council Individual Artist Awards in poetry. In addition to writing, Remington has worked as a speech-language pathologist for the Kennedy Krieger Institute and the Baltimore City Public Schools. She currently teaches poetry writing at Towson University and lives in Catonsville, Maryland, with her husband and two sons.

About CityLit Press

CityLit Press's mission is to provide a venue for writers who might otherwise be overlooked by larger publishers due to the literary nature or regional focus of their projects. It is the imprint of nonprofit CityLit Project, founded in Baltimore in 2004.

CityLit nurtures the culture of literature in Baltimore and throughout Maryland by creating enthusiasm for literature, building a community of avid readers and writers. Thank you to our major supporters: the National Endowment for the Arts, the Maryland State Arts Council, the Baltimore Office of Promotion and The Arts, and the Baltimore Community Foundation. More information and documentation is available at www.guidestar.org.

Additional support is provided by individual contributors. Financial support is vital for sustaining the ongoing work of the organization. Secure on-line donations can by made at our web site (click on "Donate").

CityLit is a member of the Greater Baltimore Cultural Alliance, the Maryland Association of Nonprofit Organizations, Maryland Citizens for the Arts, and the Writers' Conferences and Centers division of the Association of Writing Programs (AWP).

For submission guidelines, information about CityLit Press's poetry chapbook contest, and public programs offered by CityLit, please visit www.citylitproject.org.

ART WORKS.
arts.gov

MARYLAND
STATE ARTS
COUNCIL

BALTIMORE
OFFICE OF PROMOTION & THE ARTS

B C F
BALTIMORE
COMMUNITY
FOUNDATION

About the Harriss Poetry Prize

Launched in 2009 under the guidance of poet and CityLit Project chair Michael Salcman, the Harriss Poetry Prize is named in honor of Clarinda Harriss, eminent Baltimore poet, publisher, and professor of English at Towson University. Harriss, educated at Johns Hopkins University and Goucher College, is a widely published, award-winning poet and she serves as director of BrickHouse Books, Maryland's oldest literary press, which *Baltimore* magazine named "Best of Baltimore."

2013 Judge: Marie Howe
2012 Judge: Tom Lux
2011 Judge: Dick Allen
2010 Judge: Michael Salcman

For complete guidelines, please go to www.citylitproject.org and click on "CityLit Press." Send entry fee, manuscript with table of contents, acknowledgments, and two coversheets (one with name, title, mailing address, daytime phone, and email address and one with title only) to:

Harriss Poetry Prize
CityLit Press
c/o CityLit Project
120 S. Curley Street
Baltimore, MD 21224

Annual submission deadline is October 1 (postmarked).

CITYLIT
PRESS

5th Annual
Harriss Poetry Prize
Judge: Afaa Michael Weaver

PAST WINNERS

Rebekah Remington
Judged by
Marie Howe

Katherine Bogden
Judged by
Tom Lux

Bruce Sager
Judged by
Dick Allen

Laura Shovan
Judged by
Michael Salcman

$500 Prize
Plus Publication and 50 Copies

Postmark: October 1
Please see complete submission
guidelines on-line. CityLit Press is the
imprint of CityLit Project.

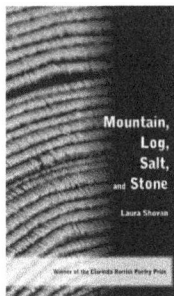

Katherine Bogden   Bruce Sager   Laura Shovan